Lin Lin Pangolin

NIGHTINGALE PAPERBACK
© Copyright 2020
Catherine Jenkins
Illustrations by Jayne Ruffell-Ward

A CIP catalogue record for this title is
available from the British Library.
ISBN 978 1 83875 005 3

*Nightingale Books is an imprint of
Pegasus Elliot MacKenzie Publishers Ltd.*
www.pegasuspublishers.com

First Published in 2020
Nightingale Books
Sheraton House Castle Park
Cambridge England
Printed & Bound in Great Britain

Catherine Jenkins

Lin Lin Pangolin

Nightingale Books

It is April in the Chinese Emerald Forest.
Lin Lin Pangolin sleeps soundly.
She is only two weeks old.
Lin Lin slowly wakes and opens her sleepy little eyes.

Crunch, crunch, crunch.
Mother Pangolin walks through the luscious leafy undergrowth carrying Lin Lin safely on her strong, scaly tail.

Lin Lin smells the dark scent of the chocolate crumbly earth…
the sweet scent of the leafy emerald foliage…
and the delicate perfume of the candy-pink camellias.
She feels the gentle brush of bamboo leaves
as she is carried safely through the Emerald Forest.

Shhh! What's that noise?
Crunch… Boom! Crunch… Boom! Crunch… Boom!

An ENORMOUS grey, flappy-eared elephant
comes lolloping through the bamboo.

PHEW!

Mother Pangolin walks on and
stumbles upon a round mound of earth.
Excitedly, she digs the mound using her five large claws.
She has no teeth but uses her extremely long and super-sticky
tongue to extract the tasty, tongue-tickling termites.
Mother Pangolin stays for a long time
clawing and scraping and sticking and licking.

Finally, after much feeding, she continues on her way.
Mother is thirsty after eating all of those tasty treats.
She sniffs her way through the bamboo and down
to the sparkling fresh water of the forest lake.

Shhh! What's that noise?
Splosh! Slurp. Splosh! Slurp. Splosh! Slurp.

Amongst the bamboo, at the edge of the lake, a fluffy black and white panda sits cupping water in his GINORMOUS paws.

PHEW!

Mother Pangolin laps up the sweet clear water,
using her long, slender tongue.
After drinking plenty, she continues on her way
making the long climb back up into the deep forest.

Shhh! What's that noise?
He-He-He!   He-He-He!   He-He-He!

Lin Lin looks up.
Above, golden snub-nosed monkeys laugh
as they zoom from branch to branch through the trees.

PHEW!

They finally reach the top of the hill and are almost home.
Lin Lin is starting to feel sleepy after her
adventurous day of new scents, sights, and sounds.
She's getting hungry too…

Shhh! What's that noise?
Rustle… Crack! Rustle… Crack! Rustle… Crack!
Is it a leopard?
Is it a human?

Using her tail, Mother Pangolin quickly gathers Lin Lin onto her
soft, warm belly and folds her into a tight, snug little ball to hide her.
Eighteen rows of pangolin scales protect her from predators.
Lin Lin's scales are still very soft, but Mother Pangolin's are tough.

When the danger has passed,
Mother Pangolin unfurls to release Lin Lin into the sparkling sunshine.
She climbs back onto her mother's strong, scaly tail
and they continue on their journey home.

Inside the burrow, snug and safe,
Mother Pangolin gently releases Lin Lin from her tail
and onto the warm, chocolate earth.

Lin Lin is hungry!
Lin Lin will not be able to eat termites until she is one month old.
For now she loves settling down with Mother Pangolin
and suckling her deliciously sweet and creamy milk
and then…

she soundly sleeps.

Pangolins, or scaly anteaters, are extraordinary animals. They are the world's only truly scaly mammals and their unique behaviours include scooping up ants and termites with their incredibly long, sticky tongues and curling up into a ball when threatened. There are eight species in total – four in Africa and four in Asia.

Sadly, pangolins are the most illegally traded wild mammals on the planet. They are considered a delicacy and are poached for their meat while their scales are used in traditional Asian medicine.

A proportion of the proceeds of this book will be donated to the IUCN SSC Pangolin Specialist Group, who are leading the effort to save pangolins from poaching and illegal trade. For more information about their work, please visit www.pangolinsg.org.

The following charities are also involved in pangolin conservation. Please support them if you can.
Rare & Endangered Species Trust (www.restnamibia.org)
Creative Conservation Alliance (www.conservationalliance.org)
TRAFFIC (traffic.org)

Photo Credit: Scott Trageser/NatureStills LLC

Photo Credit: Gary Ades/KFBG

Catherine Jenkins (1973 - 2019)

About the Author

Catherine grew up in London with a passion for dance and a love of nature. Both were integral to her life; she taught dance and studied zoology before going on to work in primary education.

In 2018, Catherine volunteered at Cambridge's Museum of Zoology and discovered the plight of the pangolin. She felt compelled to help raise the profile of this endangered animal and, consequently, the idea for this book was born.

Shortly after completing the manuscript, Catherine died of cancer. Fortunately she had outlined her vision to the illustrator, Jayne, who realised it so beautifully. Catherine would be thrilled with how the sensitive illustrations relay her story.